Bulletproof Backbone

Abhijit Naskar is a celebrated Neuroscientist, Bestselling Author of 100+ books, and the World's Beloved Poet of 1000+ sonnets, who has been serving at the forefront of humankind's struggle against hate, intolerance, bigotry and fanaticism.

Bulletproof
BACKBONE

Injustice Not Allowed
on My Watch

ABHIJIT
NASKAR

Also by Abhijit Naskar

The Art of Neuroscience in Everything
Your Own Neuron: A Tour of Your Psychic Brain
The God Parasite: Revelation of Neuroscience
The Spirituality Engine
Love Sutra: The Neuroscientific Manual of Love
Homo: A Brief History of Consciousness
Neurosutra: The Abhijit Naskar Collection
Autobiography of God: Biopsy of A Cognitive Reality
Biopsy of Religions: Neuroanalysis towards Universal
Tolerance
Prescription: Treating India's Soul
What is Mind?
In Search of Divinity: Journey to The Kingdom of Conscience
Love, God & Neurons: Memoir of a scientist who found
himself by getting lost
The Islamophobic Civilization: Voyage of Acceptance
Neurons of Jesus: Mind of A Teacher, Spouse & Thinker
Neurons, Oxygen & Nanak
The Education Decree
Principia Humanitas
The Krishna Cancer
Rowdy Buddha: The First Sapiens
We Are All Black: A Treatise on Racism
The Bengal Tigress: A Treatise on Gender Equality
Either Civilized or Phobic: A Treatise on Homosexuality
Wise Mating: A Treatise on Monogamy
Illusion of Religion: A Treatise on Religious
Fundamentalism
The Film Testament
Human Making is Our Mission: A Treatise on Parenting
I Am The Thread: My Mission
7 Billion Gods: Humans Above All
Lord is My Sheep: Gospel of Human
Morality Absolute
A Push in Perception
Let The Poor Be Your God
Conscience over Nonsense
Saint of The Sapiens
Time to Save Medicine

Fabric of Humanity
Build Bridges not Walls: In the name of Americana
The Constitution of The United Peoples of Earth
Lives to Serve Before I Sleep
When Humans Unite: Making A World Without Borders
All For Acceptance
Monk Meets World
Mission Reality
Citizens of Peace: Beyond The Savagery of Sovereignty
Operation Justice: To Make A Society That Needs No Law
See No Gender
The Gospel of Technology
Every Generation Needs Caretakers: The Gospel of
Patriotism
Aşkanjali: The Sufi Sermon
Mad About Humans: World Maker's Almanac
Revolution Indomable
When Call The People: My World My Responsibility
No Foreigner Only Family
Hurricane Humans: Give me accountability, I'll give you
peace
Ain't Enough to Look Human
Servitude is Sanctitude
Time To End Democracy: The Meritocratic Manifesto
I Vicdansaadet Speaking: No Rest Till The World is Lifted
Boldly Comes Justice: Sentient not Silent
Good Scientist: When Science and Service Combine
Sleepless for Society
Neden Türk: The Gospel of Secularism
Martyr Meets World: To Solve The Hard Problem of
Inhumanity
The Shape of A Human: Our America Their America
When Veins Ignite: Either Integration or Degradation
Heart Force One: Need No Gun to Defend Society
Solo Standing on Guard: Life Before Law
Generation Corazon: Nationalism is Terrorism
Mucize Insan: When The World is Family
Hometown Human: To Live For Soil and Society
Girl Over God: The Novel
Gente Mente Adelante: Prejudice Conquered is World
Conquered
Earthquakin' Egalitarian: I Die Everyday So Your Children
Can Live
Giants in Jeans: 100 Sonnets of United Earth

Vatican Virus: The Forbidden Fiction (Abi Naskar
Adventures Book 2)
Karadeniz Chronicle: The Novel (Abi Naskar Adventures
Book 3)
Şehit Sevda Society: Even in Death I Shall Live
Handcrafted Humanity: 100 Sonnets For A Blunderful
World
Mücadele Muhabbet: Gospel of An Unarmed Soldier
Making Britain Civilized: How to Gain Readmission to The
Human Race
Dervish Advaitam: Gospel of Sacred Feminines and Holy
Fathers
Honor He Wrote: 100 Sonnets For Humans Not Vegetables
The Gentalist: There's No Social Work, Only Family Work
Either Reformist or Terrorist: If You Are Terror I Am Your
Grandfather
Woman Over World: The Novel (Abi Naskar Adventures
Book 4)
High Voltage Habib: Gospel of Undoctrination
Bulldozer on Duty
Find A Cause Outside Yourself: Sermon of Sustainability
Ingan Impossible: Handbook of Hatebusting
Amor Apocalypse: Canım Sana İhtiyacım
Amantes Assemble: 100 Sonnets of Servant Sultans
Mucize Misafir Merhaba: The Peace Testament
Divane Dynamite: Only truth in the cosmos is love
Sin Dios Sí Hay Divinidad: The Pastor Who Never Was
Corazon Calamidad: Obedient to None, Oppressive to None
Esperanza Impossible: 100 Sonnets of Ethics, Engineering &
Existence
Mukemmel Musalman: Kafir Biraz, Peygamber Biraz
Himalayan Sonneteer: 100 Sonnets of Unsubmission
Yarasistan: My Wounds, My Crown
The Centurion Sermon: Mental Por El Mundo
Her Insan Ailem: Everyone is Family, Everywhere is Home
Humankind, My Valentine: World's First Anthology of 1000
Sonnets
Naskar's Knights: The Humanitarian Omnibus
Aşk Mafia: Armor of The World
Vande Vasudhaivam: 100 Sonnets for Our Planetary Pueblo
Visvavictor: Kanima Akiyor Kainat
Sapionova: 200 Limericks for Students
Rowdy Scientist: Handbook of Humanitarian Science
Insan Himalayanoğlu: It's Time to Defect

Tum Dunya Tek Millet: Greatest Country on Earth is Earth
Either Right or Human: 300 Limericks of Inclusion
Yaralardan Yangın Doğar: Explorers of Night are Emperors
of Dawn

DEDICATION

To Palestine.

"Al-Shams to Alpha Centauri,
All occupied lands will be free.
Till there is smile on every face,
All happiness is blasphemy."

CONTENTS

1. Sapiosultan Sonnet

Sapiosultan
(The Sonnet, 1267)

They ask me, do I believe in destiny?
Sure, I do - you are looking at it.
I am destiny - of you - of the world,
I am the destiny of entire humanity.

I am the bridge - between everything -
science, poetry, philosophy - everything.
Between everything and everyone -
I am the bridge between hearts still beating.

I am not a servant to the field,
I am a servant to the valley -
the valley of life and light -
beyond the squabbles of dead sanity.

Who am I - or better yet, what am I?
I am but a spark of reason tempered by warmth,
I am but a spark of boldness tempered by humility,
I am but a spark of justice tempered by conscience.

I am neither man nor woman,
I am neither mind nor machine,
I am neither head nor heart,
I am neither spine nor spleen.

I am but that - that one ceaseless truth,
aspiring across all fallacies untrue.

I am but that - that one untainted light,
shining as proof of time yet to come true.
Sabiosultan, El Soneto

Me preguntan ¿creo en el destino?
Claro que sí, lo estás mirando.
Yo soy el destino, de la humanidad;
Yo soy el destino del mundo entero.

Yo soy el puente – entre todo,
Ciencia, poesía, filosofía, todo.
Yo soy el puente entre todo y todos,
Soy el puente entre corazones vivos.

No soy un siervo del intelecto,
No soy un siervo de la tradición.
Soy un soldado del valle de la vida,
Más allá de las riñas del sentido muerto.

¿Quién soy? O mejor aún, ¿qué soy?
Soy una chispa de razón templada por la calidez.
Yo soy valentía atemperada por la humildad,
Yo soy la justicia atemperada por la conciencia.

No soy ni hombre ni mujer,
No soy ni mente ni máquina;
No soy ni cabeza ni corazón,
No soy ni cuerpo ni columna.

Sólo soy esa - esa verdad eterna,
Que supera todos los prejuicios y falacias.
Sólo soy esa - esa luz incorruptible,

Que brilla como prueba de la humanidad unida.

Yeni Zaman, Yeni Paşa
(Kalpkomutan Şiir)

Bana soruyor ki - kadere güveniyor musun?
Neden güvenmeyeyim - tabii ki güveniyorum.
Her an, her dakika, kaderin sonucudur,
Ve dünyanın kaderini ben yazıyorum.

Zafer yok, zeka yok, yine de umurumda değil;
Hiç kötü kader amacımı bozamaz benim.
Korku ve köktencilik kavgalarının ötesinde,
İnatçı bir aşk umudu, desteğimdir benim.

Ben kimim - neyim - biliyor musun?
Acılar denizinde ilacın ışığıyım ben.
Nefretin ortasında niyetin kıvılcımıyım,
Hayvanlığın ortasında insanlığın cevabı ben.

Kalbim benim dünyanın ilahi bir köprüsüdür;
Her hayat, her hikmet, kalbimde yaşıyor.
Hayatım benim dünyaya verilen bir hediyedir;
Her dil, din ve kültür, kalbimde birleşiyor.

2. Myth of Nonviolence

Nonviolence is nonsense – or to be more accurate – bookish nonviolence is nonsense. It's a myth. Nonviolence is to injustice, what homeopathy is to illness – it claims all the credit without any of the responsibility. Placebo brings comfort, not change.

Does that mean, violence is the solution? That's the problem, you see. This prehistoric world has an instinctual affinity to black and white concepts – to binary concepts – and a gigantic blind spot for grey areas. Justice is too grand an exercise to be contained by the primitive dualistic nonsense of violence and nonviolence.

Let me put this into perspective with an example. Bullets are an act of violence, silence is an act of nonviolence – but there is a third option – the option of the slipper.

Slippers are more effective in fighting bugs, than bullets – bullets make martyr of the bugs, slippers put them in their place. When the slippers of a nation's civilians combine, even the mightiest of tyrant is bound to fall – be it a state head, court judge or law enforcement officer.

Whenever a bunch of bugs turn the courts into a cradle of animal masculinity – whenever a bunch of bugs turn the parliament into a cradle of fundamentalism and bigotry – whenever a bunch of bugs turn the police stations into a cradle of badge-bearing barbarism – grab hold of that household bug-repellent you wear on your feet, and put them to some good, wholesome use. Treat the corrupt and bigoted like your children, and do with them as you would your own child when they go astray.

When your child starts to bully other kids, if you adopt pacifism and pamper them further in the name of nonviolence, instead of taking stringent steps to nip their megalomania in the bud, it's very much possible, they might grow up to be the next orange-haired terrorist to roam the oval office or the next musky moron who takes pleasure in destroying people's livelihoods and providing safe haven to hate speech and disinformation to satisfy their giant ego and puny mind.

So, I repeat – pick up the democratic superweapon from under your feet and put it to good use – treat the privileged orangutans like your children and put them in their rightful place, without actually harming them. Your world, your rules – remember that. Slippers are democracy's first line of defense, bullets it's last.

3. Past Excuse

Nonviolence is nonsense, just like spirituality is nonsense. You heard right. Spirituality is supposed to be an act of self awareness – an act of self-discovery - instead it has become a domain of new-age superstitions – just like, nonviolence is supposed to be an exercise in love, instead it has become an excuse for indifference and inaction.

This won't do - this won't do no more.

Justice begins with a just person - an unbending person - an unbigoted person. Or to put it another way - justice begins when indifference ends - knowledge begins when rigidity ends.

Pay attention to this one word - rigidity - for that's the root of all the troubles in the world - that's the seed of all the barriers in the world - all the walls in the world - walls between mind and mind - between life and life - between people and people. Treat rigidity and you treat all social illnesses in the world.

All roads lead to people - those that don't, lead back to the jungle. And this is possible only when your heart is hateproof.

Biasproof your brain, bulletproof your backbone, hateproof your heart. Till hate is history, there is no human history, there is only animal history. And how do we initiate that human history - by recognizing the animal within. Only when you are aware of the animal you are, you can take charge of the human you want to be.

4. Final Human (The Sonnet)

Final Human
(The Sonnet, 1268)

Only animal I'm afraid of is myself,
When I'm scared, I lose control.
I am the height of violence extreme,
Kept tamed by conscience whole.

I am the maker of all law and order,
I decide what's right, what's wrong.
I am a grenade waiting to go off,
At the sight of humanity done wrong.

To the helpless I'm humility incarnate,
To the discriminated I'm love unbound.
To all intolerance I am judgment day,
To paranoid hate I'm piety paramount.

If I don't bulldoze your castles of prejudice,
Abhijit Vicdansaadet Naskar is not my name.
Till the last ounce of hate is obliterated,
The final human will emerge time and again.

5. I am Justice Absolute

Where there is a human, there is love - where there is a human, there is liberty - where there is a human, there is justice. It's not about a certain bookish theory - it's not about a certain ideology, it's not about a certain philosophy - it's just about being human - it's about a human behaving human - alive and accountable.

The vessel and the name are irrelevant;
Till all hate is obliterated,
the force within will keep emerging
over and over again.

I have zero tolerance for intolerance,
But don't consider this as a threat.
I'm merely declaring the parameters,
Of the cosmic limits of human tolerance.

What do you take me for - some two-bit frozen figurine from the icy-cold world of intellect! Armageddon here! Armageddon above intellect - armageddon above faith - armageddon above law, order and policy!

I am Justice absolute - Jehovah absolute - Jehennem (Hell) absolute! I am Conscience absolute - Christ absolute - Cosmos absolute! I am Harmony absolute - Human absolute - Heaven absolute!

I am the first prophet and the last - I am the keeper of eternity. I am time, I am space - I am the beginning of love, and the obliteration of inhumanity.

Every time this prehistoric world even dreams of tyranny, bearing its political, bureaucratic, legal, or religious badge of authoritarianism, remember who you are. You are brahmanda (cosmos) in a brain - you are the first, second and last coming - you are the one who parted Red Sea - you are but consciousness dawning.

6. Thousand Naskars (The Sonnet)

Thousand Naskars
(The Sonnet, 1269)

When one Naskar dies in body,
Thousand Naskars will take his place.
Cowards seek comfort in reincarnation,
While the brave step in to fill the void.

Don't you dare make a cult of me,
Waiting for yet another second coming!
Reclaim your life from the land of myths,
Wishful inaction is most unbecoming.

Charge up your mind with facts and reason,
Charge up your heart with love and vision.
Backbone alive repels cowardly inaction,
Even if peddled by thousand year tradition.

When one Naskar dies in body,
Thousand Naskars will take his place.
Naskar the person died a long time ago,
What speaks to you is Naskar the oneness.

7. When You Raise Terrorists

I don't care if my blood
courses through your veins,
I only care whether my ideas
electrify your nerves.
I don't give a damn
if I leave no bloodly offspring,
my sole objective is to
leave behind godly bravehearts.

My soldiers don't need guns,
My soldiers don't need bombs.
Their backbone is power enough,
To electrify their struggle upward.

You keep buying your children toy pistols, then you wonder, why there is no peace in the world! When you raise terrorists, you are bound to have terrorism - most of which is democratically glorified as patriotism. It takes just one generation of parents to put an end to the prehistoric tradition of war and hate - just one generation. So, my question is - are you that generation? Only parents can end wars, not politicians - only education can end terror, not armament.

Les compras pistolas de juguete a tus hijos y luego te preguntas por qué no hay paz en el mundo. Cuando se crían terroristas, seguramente tendrás terrorismo - que en su mayoría se glorifica como patriotismo. Sólo hace falta una generación de madres y padres para poner fin a la tradición prehistórica de guerra y odio - solamente una generación. Entonces mi pregunta es ¿eres de esa generación? Sólo las madres y los padres pueden poner fin a las guerras, no los políticos - sólo la educación puede acabar con el terror, no el armamento.

Policy changes nothing, if the everyday habits of the people that breed all the uncharitable feelings in the world, remain the same. Change policy, you change the world for a few years. Change habits, you change the world for good.

8. Patriotism is Primitiveness

Patriotism might have been a civilized inspiration in the past - but in the context of modern times, patriotism is primitiveness. Patriotism is the antithesis of world peace - it is the antithesis of acceptance, integration and harmony - in short, patriotism is the ultimate crime against humanity. Let me show you how.

What's the image that comes to your mind, when you hear the word "patriotism"? A soldier with a gun - and where there is a soldier, there is an enemy. And who is that enemy? Usually it's just another soldier from the other side of the border - who has his own children, own spouse, own family at home, and is the symbol of patriotism in his own nation. Now, do you see the absurdity of the whole concept of patriotism! That's how sick this society is - where the only thing that distinguishes patriotism from terrorism is which side of the border bears your feet shackled - borders that are peddled by politicians to maintain control - not security, not peace, but control. Because a world without borders is a world without fear - and it's impossible to control people when they no longer fear each other.

Even if I accept your bogus excuses for war, today we have the technology to fight wars without actually killing people - only reason we don't, is because it's not economical. Life is not economical, death is - peace is not economical, war is. It's far cheaper to kill enemy soldiers than take them prisoner, at the expense of the taxpayer. One bullet costs half a dollar, whereas one prisoner costs thousands per year. So, naturally, preserving life is not the priority, neither is peace. Besides, think of the rush of pride the primitive taxpayers get, from the headlines - "our nation's gallant forces took down several enemy soldiers in a bone-chilling surgical strike!" And more the primitives of a nation are exposed to this kind of blood-boiling headlines, more they get conditioned to believe, that in every war, they are on the right side of justice. World calls it Geopolitics - I call it Pavlovian Conditioning of Patriotism - where the citizen canines of a state are made to believe even the worst of stately atrocity to be just and righteous, by repeated exposure of a patriotic narrative. As I once said, whoever controls the narrative, controls the people. And fear is at the root of it all. Once the citizens conquer their fear and prejudice, and grow up into civilized thinking humans, that'll be the end of state, war and geopolitical tribalism.

So, the question is, how do you fix all this nonsense?

Simple - you gotta write your own constitution, you gotta develop your own culture, you gotta be a government unto yourself.

Say out loud.

Conscience is my constitution,
Compassion is my culture,
Character is my government.
I don't need any second hand
constitution, second hand culture,
second hand government.

9. Fossil Fuel is Not The Problem

Neither fossil fuel nor artificial intelligence is the problem - the real danger is greed. Do you think everybody will live happily ever after, once you replace fossil fuel with green energy! No - they won't! Apekind will simply use green energy to power their greed instead of oil and gas. They will use green energy to wage war, they'll use green energy to kill people. US military is already developing a high-endurance unmanned solar powered aircraft, to be used as a communication relay platform and for surveillance. Besides, solar powered reconnaissance drones have already been in military use for some years now, in various parts of the world. Which means, the planet will be safer, but the people will be in just as much muck as they are today.

Apparently, there is a limit to fossil fuel, but there is no limit to human stupidity. Apekind will find one way or another to continue with their "kill or be killed" nonsense, just like any other animal in the wild. And every time government officials will make the same old statement, "it's necessary for national security"

- just as power hungry tribal chiefs have been saying since our jungle days, before putting millions upon millions to death!

So, my question is - what good is green energy if it's used for the same inhuman purposes as fossil fuel!

Treat greed first, you fools - treat greed first! Then you won't need to make a ton of empty promises and winded policies for a sustainable future - because where there is no greed, sustainability flows like spring water. Treat greed first, then I shall call you humankind - until then, you are nothing but apekind. Without the green of heart, what green apes, what oil apes - all energy leads to but one color - the color of blood - red! Energy used to sustain the same old paradigm of greed, control and disparity, is anything but clean - no matter what it says on the label.

10. Past Intolerance

It is in the absence of the green of heart, that fundamentalism and nationalism manage to rip this world apart. However, despite historic records, fundamentalism and nationalism are not an American issue or European issue, it's a human issue. The savage elements of intolerance and divisionism are found all over the world, because it's rooted in our universally primeval animal nature. That's why, intolerance is not really a white problem or black problem, it's a human problem. Let me show you how.

Fanatics of India, for example, keep claiming, India is a Hindu nation, and yet - India's Icon of Science was a Muslim, India's greatest architectural wonder of love is a mausoleum - and take away love and science from a society, and what's left? Nothing.

All this is possible because India is a secular nation. Among all the ancient civilizations, only India has sustained herself as a secular nation, despite the eternal resistance of savages. The day India stops being secular, she'll stop being India.

You see, there is no such thing as Hinduism - the actual phrase is Sanatana Dharma, which is not a religion, but an everyday sense of oneness or advaita - which is the very backbone of the Indian society. Only in India people celebrate Eid with as much enthusiasm as they celebrate Diwali - they celebrate Christmas with as much enthusiasm as they celebrate Nanak Jayanti - and that's Sanatana Dharma for you.

And had Subhas Chandra Bose not died in a plane crash at the front, had Bhagat Singh not been hanged by the British, and had Gandhi not been killed by a Hindu extremist moron, Bharat, Pakistan and Bangladesh together would be shining as the brightest beacon of multiculturalism on the face of earth, rather than being torn into pieces by the glorious barbarians of the British Empire.

Anyway, the point is this. Sanatana Dharma or Ancient Duty is not a religion, it's the absolute integration of religions. If you wanna study innovation, study America, or better yet, study China - but if you wanna study integration, study India.

So, I repeat - there is no Hinduism, there is only Oneness or Advaita - just like there is no Catholicism or C of E, there is only "Love Thy Neighbor" - there is no Judaism, there is only Ahava.

When you lose touch with "love thy neighbor", you end up with christian nationalism - when you lose touch with advaita or nonduality, you end up with hindutva - when you lose touch with ahava, you end up with zionism.

11. Statement on Hamas

When Israel strikes, it's "national security" - when Palestine strikes back, it's "terrorism". Just like over two hundred years ago when native americans resisted their homeland being stolen, it was called "Indian Attack". Or like over a hundred years ago when Indian soldiers in the British Army revolted against the empire, in defense of their homeland, it was called "Sepoy Mutiny".

The narrative never changes - when the colonizer terrorizes the world, it's given glorious sounding names like "exploration" and "conquest", but if the oppressed so much as utters a word in resistance, it is branded as attack, mutiny and terrorism - so that, the real terrorists can keep on colonizing as the self-appointed ruler of land, life and morality, without ever being held accountable for violating the rights of what they deem second rate lifeforms, such as the arabs, indians, latinos and so on.

After all this, some apes will still only be interested in one stupid question. Do I support Hamas? To which I say this. Until you've spent a lifetime under an oppressive regime, you are not qualified to ask that question. An ape can ask anything its puny brain fancies, but it's up to the human to decide whether the ape is worthy of a response. What do you think, by the way - colonizers can just keep coming as they please, to wipe their filthy feet on us like doormat, and we should do nothing - just stay quiet! For creatures who call themselves civilized, you guys have a weird sense of morality.

Yet all these might not get through your thick binary skull, so let me put it to you bluntly.

I don't stand with Hamas, I am Hamas, just like, I don't stand with Ukraine, I am Ukraine. Russia stops fighting, war ends - Ukraine stops fighting, Ukraine ends. Israel ends invasion, war ends - Palestine ends resistance, Palestine ends.

However, I do have one problem here. Why do civilians have to die, if that is indeed the case - which I have no way of confirming, because news reports are not like reputed scientific data, that a scientist can naively trust. During humankind's gravest conflicts news outlets have always peddled a narrative benefiting the occupier and demonizing the resistance, either consciously or subconsciously. So never go by news reports, particularly on exception circumstances like this.

No matter the cause, no civilian must die, that is my one unimpeachable law. But the hard and horrific fact of the matter is, only the occupier can put an end to the death and destruction peacefully - the resistance does not have that luxury.

12. The New British Empire

If the Israeli attack on Gaza has proven anything, it is that, no matter how democratic, just and progressive you think of your government to be, when things get really desperate, they always choose primitive political interest over global humanitarian interest.

I wonder - what did we really achieve by replacing the orange-haired orangutan with a better alternative, if that better alternative ultimately fails as horribly as his predecessor, when things get really desperate. I may not be a US citizen, but I am a US taxpayer, and when tax dollars from my books on peace and justice are used to aid and fund genocide and war, I find it difficult to maintain respect for such new administration. Citizens of earth could end all wars in a year - boycott all tax-filing unless your governments cease all defense activities for good.

US government is the number 1 widow-maker, orphan-maker and refugee-maker in the world, and as such, Washington DC is the ultimate war criminal of modern history.

Hence it is no surprise, when things rough, Uncle Sam would choose political interest over human rights.

Earth will thrive in the absence of humankind, Peace will prosper in the absence of US government. US government is the modern day equivalent of the British Empire. Just like, monarchy is the british equivalent of the confederacy. Those who identify with it, can't live without it, but those who are humans, know the inhumanity it represents.

You see, the United States never really broke off with the British Empire, it simply became the new age British Empire - it became the new face of tyranny, that's all.

13. No More Genocide

No guns,
No greed,
No grandeur.
Period.

No military,
No mindlessness,
No more massacre.
Enough already!

No nationalism,
No fundamentalism,
No more genocide -
Stop it, you monkeys!

When liberty is branded terrorism,
And terrorism is declared self defense,
Ceasefire is vetoed as taboo,
Geopolitics is fancy talk for arms race.

14. The Question

Couple of years back I once wrote – how come we can invent better ways to kill each other, but not one to preserve peace! Tracking back the origin of the statement I found out that, it's not from any of the books, but a part of an introduction to the Memorial Day Sonnet released on my wordpress site.

Anyway, the point is – today that question rings more evident than ever. So, I shall convey it in a few other languages in order to make it more universally organic. Because guess what – even though English is the universal language of earth, due to its primitive colonial escapades, and indeed the most convenient, it is neither the most beautiful nor the most soulful language on earth.

Therefore at this difficult humanitarian moment I say to you once again:

How come we can invent better ways to kill each other, but not one to preserve peace!

¡Cómo es que podemos inventar mejores maneras de matarnos unos a otros, pero ninguna para preservar la paz!

Come mai possiamo inventare modi migliori per ucciderci a vicenda, ma non uno per preservare la pace!

Nasıl yani, birbirimizi öldürmenin binlerce yol biliyoruz, ama barışı korumanın bir tane bile yok!

نبتكر أن يمكننا كيف البعض، بعضنا لقتل أفضل طرقاً نجد ولا
!االسلام على للحفاظ طريقة

انسانيت، ايمان

محبت؛ مذہب

نہیں، کی خون

چاہت۔ ہے کی امن

Hur kommer det sig att vi kan uppfinna bättre sätt att döda varandra, men inte ett sätt att bevara freden!

Wie kommt es, dass wir bessere Wege finden können, um einander zu töten, aber nicht um den Frieden zu bewahren!

15. The Memo

Memo to The States of Earth: *All through time, the conquerors have been writing history. But no more! The conquerors are no longer the supreme emperor of the narrative, even if all the spineless governments take their side. Because guess what - society is no longer a property of the state. You ask us to vaccinate, we shall vaccinate - you ask us to follow traffic rules, we shall follow traffic rules - you ask us to file our taxes, we shall file our taxes - because that's the civilized thing to do. But if you ask us to support your rich moron of a friend in his exploits of conquest and domination, you shall not have a government to begin with. Remember that.*

You see, world history has always revolved around the benefit of the colonizer - that too, under the glorious banner of civilization. And anyone who put a damper on their glorious plan was branded a villain. Most times these villains were actual heroes of true civilization, fighting for real liberty - but from time to time the villain was really a villain, even though their villainy were nothing compared to the predominant villainy of the colonizers.

16. Hitler is Nothing

How come Hitler is a bigger villain than the British monarchy, when Hitler invaded only 11 countries, while the British empire invaded 90 percent of the globe, that is, over 170 countries, and caused multiple times the massacre than the Nazis did! And while modern Germans are well aware of the nation's horrific past, and try their best to right the wrongs, like civilized, conscientious humans ought to, in barbarian britain however, over half the population still stand proudly behind the monarchy, let alone recognize the animal filth it represents, which till this day is unparalleled by any other animal regime.

Now to the reason why Hitler is officially a villain, but not the British monarchy. Hitler invaded white countries, while the British empire invaded mostly colored countries - and since colored life is cheap, but white life is priceless, Hitler is branded a villain, while the Brits are designated "explorers" and "bringers of civilization", a tradition which has been proudly inherited by the modern day British Empire - the United States of America.

The point is, you cannot do the right thing, till you know what you've been doing wrong. Or to put it simpler still - you cannot be human, till you know what's inhuman.

And for those who still cannot fathom the simple act of being human, let me put it in a nursery rhyme!

Repeat after me.

Twinkle twinkle little star,
I know exactly what you are.
Nursery rhyme for humankind,
Descending all from Africa.

17. Black History Sonnet

Offsprings of Africa
(Black History Sonnet, 1270)

If a black family lives
long enough in a cold climate,
in about 100 generations or so,
their descendants will be born white.

This is how the white people were born,
Because we all come from a black mother.
No matter where we live on earth,
We're all Africans - our homeland, Africa.

Till you get this anthropological fact,
You are but a traitor to earth.
Black History is World History,
We are all offsprings of Africa.

Descendientes de África
(Soneto de la Historia Negra)

Si una familia negra vive
lo suficiente en un clima frío,
en aproximadamente 100 generaciones,
sus descendientes nacerán blancos.

Así nacieron los blancos,
Porque todos venimos de una madre negra.
No importa dónde vivamos en la tierra,
Somos todos africanos - nuestra patria, África.

Si no comprendes este hecho antropológico,
No eres más que un traidor a la tierra.
La historia negra es historia mundial,
Somos todos descendientes de África.

18. Culture and State

Africa is the mother of all cultures. If we go back long enough, all cultures would converge in Africa. And yet, oblivious to our singular origin, we keep fighting with each other over whose culture is superior to the other. And the so-called modern geopolitical landscape does nothing to ease this tension - if anything, it only facilitates them, in name of national identity - because even by accident, if the people of earth learn to behave human, all politicians and governments will be out of business - and there will be no trace of any state and nation, only humanity and earth.

All governments use cultural heritage to guilt trap their citizens into remaining tribal sheep. However, culture and state are two completely different phenomena - the former involves everyday life of people, the later involves control of people.

That's why I say to you - never confuse culture with state. Some of the richest cultures of the world often end up with some of the most regressive states in the world - Türkiye,

Azerbaijan, India, Italy to name a few, in the context of 2023.

So I repeat, never let your disapproval of a government make you bitter towards a culture. Government never reflects culture - if it did, I would not have penned a single Turkish word in my works - as opposed to the fact that, the Turkish culture is an intrinsic element of Naskarean literature.

Also, while we are on the subject of my writing, I must address a minor issue, which I've been overlooking for a while now.

Across the globe I am often referred to as "the Indian neuroscientist" or "the Indian Author", despite the fact that my work is practically nonexistent in India, statistically speaking. Considering that, 90% of my book sales come from US, UK and Canada, the rest 10% from Europe, Mexico, South America and Australia, and zero from India - for transparency and context purposes I'll tell to you one more time - Abhijit Naskar is an Earth Scientist - Abhijit Naskar is an Earth Poet - Abhijit Naskar is an Earth Philosopher.

However, it's never about the sales, it's about the love. I only mention the demographics to put things in perspective. For example, there are many countries where people cannot afford to buy my books, since they are expensively exported from US and Europe, and yet, I receive far more love from these countries than the land I was born in. Philippines and Pakistan to name a few. As a matter of fact, hate wise speaking, Philippines is the only country so far, where I have not faced any hate and bigotry - which only goes to prove that, state of a currency does not reflect the broadness of heart. That's why, a substantial portion of my work is available freely on the internet.

The point is - I am no more Indian, than I am a Yank or Canadian or Mexican or Turk or Swede or Pinoy or British or Brazilian or Egyptian or Aussie. Passport is just a glorified bus pass - nothing more. So, I repeat - I am an Earth Scientist - remember that. Nationalization of Naskar is desecration of Naskar.

19. Whole Citizen

Vazgeçmem - bu dünyadan,
benim dünyamdan vazgeçmem,
İnsanlardan vazgeçmem!
Bir Naskar gidecek,
Bin Naskar gelecek, ama,
Dünyayı hiç yalnız bırakmam!

One Naskar goes, thousand Naskars will take his place. But not anybody can be a Naskar. You gotta obliterate every last trace of sectarianism and shallowness from your mind. Burning all sectarian allegiances and cravings for luxury, to ashes, you gotta emerge a whole human being - you gotta emerge a world citizen.

By world citizen I am not talking about those insta influencers who travel the world at their parents' expense, and pretend all global, with not an ounce of substance of their own.

There's no difference between a pet that travels the world at its rich owner's expense, and a kid that travels the world at their rich parents' expense. To these canines and primates I say, grow up already. Develop some backbone and build an identity of your own by yourself.

It's one thing to travel for education, and another to make luxurious trips around the world like spoiled pets of rich parents.

Whether you are born into privilege is not up to you, but when that privilege gets to your head, you forfeit all claim to human dignity.

I am proud to say, I am the son of a laborer - a factory worker - first one to have education in my family - and the first multicultural scientist and poet in human history. Naskar is made by Naskar alone, not an industry or benefactor - or more importantly, by family wealth. I had a roof over my head, food on the table, and clothes on my back – that was more than enough.

20. Sweat Today Savor Tomorrow

I started writing with literally zero dollar in my pocket. Let me tell you how it began, because for some reason, I completely forgot a crucial event of my life when I wrote my memoir Love, God & Neurons.

I once met an American tourist at a local train in Calcutta. The first thing he asked me was, had I lived in the States? I said, no. Then how come you have an American accent - he asked. Watching movies - I said. We got chatting and he told me about a book he had recently published, a memoir. I believe, this was the cosmic event that planted the thought of writing my own books in my head - I had already started my self-education in Neurology and Psychology, and I was all determined to publish research papers on my ideas, but not books. Meeting the person somehow subconsciously shifted my focus from research papers to books.

So the journey began. And for the first few years, I made no real money from my books. Occasionally some of my books would climb the bestsellers list on amazon, like my very first book did, and that would keep the bills paid for several months. Then the invitations for talks started coming, but they too were not paid in the beginning. The organizers made all the travel arrangements, and I gave the talks for free. It's ironic and super confusing really - I remember flying business class, but I didn't have enough money to even afford a one way flight ticket, because I had already used up my royalties on other expenses.

Looking back in retrospect, it all makes sense now, but back then when I was living the struggle, it made absolutely no sense. In fact, I often asked myself, how come so many people are talking about me, yet I am still struggling! It was a different kind of struggle than that of my vagabond years, when I had no prospect whatsoever - nevertheless it was a struggle alright, and far more confusing at that - particularly the dilemma - am I successful or aren't I! I was making a name alright, but it didn't seem to reflect on my financial condition.

Today I can pick and choose which speaking invitations to accept, but back then I didn't have that luxury - I was grateful for any speaking gig and interview request I received, paid or not. One time, I gave an interview to this moderately popular journalist for her personal youtube channel, only to find out, she never released the video publicly - she posted an interview with a dog owner instead - whose dog videos had gained quite a following on social media. You could say, this was the first time I realized first hand, what white privilege was.

Anyway, the point is this.

Did I doubt myself? Often. Did I consider quitting? Occasionally. But did I actually quit? Never. And because I didn't quit, the world received a vast never-before seen multicultural humanitarian legacy, that you know me for today.

That's how it works really. There is no such thing as overnight success. If you have a dream, you gotta work at it day in, day out - night after night - spoiling sleep, ruining rest, forgetting fun. It won't be easy - far from it, it's gonna be absolutely heartbreaking - gutwrenching - you'd face doubt, confusion and devastation, every step of the way.

Bearing all that hardship if you can persist at your dream, only then in time, that dream will pave the way on its own. As I once said, the path reveals itself once you start walking.

Persist, persist, and persist, that's the only secret - there is no other. Remember this - the size of your pocket does not determine your destiny, the size of your dedication does.

Today Naskar is a humanitarian phenomenon, because Abhijit never gave up - because Abi never give up. On top of everything, I even withstood a devastating breakup along the way, still I didn't give up – if anything it only strengthened my conviction.

You see, human identity is forged from human hardship - nothing else matters. Build a life, my friend! Build a life of substance - build a life of meaning - build a life through hardship and dedication - dedication to a purpose - dedication to a goal - dedication to a dream.

Sweat today, savor tomorrow!

Work hard - work hard, my friend, so you could afford some dignity! Work hard, not to be rich, but to be self-sufficient, so that you could refuse a well-paid job on moral grounds. And most importantly keep in mind - to afford food is employment, to afford principles is success.

Have fun all you want, but that won't make life any more special than the animals in the jungle. It's the struggle that adds value to life - struggle for warmth, struggle for reason - struggle for love, light and ascension - ascension not in exterior sophistication, but in interior meaningfulness.

So, to those who care for substance over shallowness, I say - keep fun to the minimum, and learning to the maximum - focus on meaningfulness, rather than monkey-business. Remember, there is nothing braver than dedicating your life to a goal, no matter how boring it looks to wild animals.

21. Transcending Language & Culture

You can learn anything you put your heart into, as long as you have no resistance of rigidity. Rigidity is the only impediment to learning - rigidity is the greatest obstruction to growth - where there is no rigidity, there is no question of cannot. There is no cannot, there is only want not.

Let me give you an example. I can write my science and sonnets in any language I want, if I feel like it - even though I only speak about six languages. First thing I do is, spend a few days studying the grammatical structure of the language, while listening to no other language but that (via youtube). And by the end of the week my brain starts delivering its own original poetic expressions in that language - with the limited vocabulary I've absorbed during that period. This doesn't mean, I can fluently communicate in that language at this point however - that happens in about a few months along the way if I can sustain the emotional drive to continue.

That's a crucial thing for me. I cannot write in any language unless I feel an emotional pull towards that language - the longer I feel the pull, the more I write. You see, I don't need to write in all these languages of the world - those who care, will find a way. I write in more than one language because I want to. I want to leave at least something extremely personal for every culture in the world - that is, for as many cultures as I humanly can.

However in the end, the universal spirit of love, light and oneness transcends language and culture, and finds a home in the heart of every conscientious human being - and that's what counts. It's the bridge that counts, not the shape it comes in.

Someone asked me the other day - "have you ever considered winning an award?" I replied - "not really - I am a misfit - not quite mainstream enough for any of the fields. Besides, I am here to bridge cultures, not win awards. And had you really understood my work at heart, you would not be asking such meaningless questions."

22. Nuts and Bolts

I don't write for popularity, I write for posterity. But alas, the shallow cannot fathom this simple fact of life. And there is no treatment for shallowness. Even after reading the entire Summa Theologica, the shallow can only think of one primitive question - did this guy Aquinas win any award or something?

And more shallow a mind, more it craves sophistication. And today, the greatest facilitator of shallowness is technology. As a matter of fact, modern day industrialization is rooted in shallowness - hence, it feeds on shallowness.

Humanity's ghastliest disaster will not come from religious fundamentalism, it'll come from industrial fundamentalism. So, beware! Tech billionaires whom you've put on pedestal, will turn this world into a concrete jungle of nuts and bolts, driven solely by mechanical advancement and monetary profits - where except for the heirs of the world's billionaire elites, rest of humankind will live like battery hens, for they shall be expendable.

I'll put it to you plainly. Worse than the absence of technology is the presence of heartless technology. Just like, worse than the absence of knowledge is the abundance of fraudulent knowledge. For example - genius is 1% inspiration and 99% perspiration - said the genius who was 1% showman and 99% fraud.

What this means is that - you gotta be very cautious who you idolize - more importantly, above everything else, you gotta be conscious of the humane aspect of all knowledge. It's not enough to garner knowledge, we gotta develop the insight for the humane application of knowledge.

23. Sonnet 1271

Sonnet 1271

Knowledge means "know ledge",
that is, to know the limit.
Only by knowing your limit,
can you chart the course to surpass it.

But it's not enough to surpass your limit,
What's essential is to surpass as human.
Amidst the excitement of new adventures,
Never you forget, you're love elemental.

Corazón amable es corazón valiente,
Corazón valiente es corazón amable.
Amabilidad y valentía van de la mano,
Corazón cruel es corazón cobarde.

Kind heart is courageous heart,
Courageous heart is kind heart.
Bravery without kindness leads to brutality,
Cruel heart is a cowardly heart.

Courage alone doesn't make the human,
Knowledge alone doesn't make the human.
Without heart all these are useless,
Without heart all dare is decadence.

24. Viva la Familia Mundial (Soneto)

¡Viva la Familia Mundial!
(Soneto 1142*)

Naskar el científico dice que,
La ciencia que no eleva
la condición humana,
no es ciencia, es superstición.
Naskar el monje dice que,
La inclusión es iluminación,
la discriminación es engaño.

Naskar el filósofo dice que,
Es mejor perder la verdad
que perder la humanidad -
Es mejor perder la verdad
que perder el amor.
Naskar el sufí dice que,
Siéntete a ti mismo hasta que
no sientas nada pero el amor.

Naskar el humanista dice que,
No me importa tu creencia o incredulidad,
solo importa, tu comportamiento con los demás.
Naskar el humanitario dice que,
Los humanos debemos ganarnos nuestra admisión
en la raza humana con acciones humanas.

El espíritu de amor habla de amor,
más allá de toda fe y razón;
El odio es sólo una señal de estrechez.

Cuando te expandes en corazón y alma,
el mundo entero se vuelve pariente.

(*This is the spanish version of Sonnet 1142 from
"Vande Vasudhaivam: 100 Sonnets for Our
Planetary Pueblo")

25. Bulldozerlike

> Dare to be human accountable,
> not to be animal reckless.
> Dare to practice magnanimity,
> not to be merchant of malice.

One day my memories will fade, but the world's memory of me will never fade - that's how I've lived my life. Pick a purpose, then live with a bulldozerlike dedication to that purpose, obliterating every obstruction that comes your way, and in time, your existence will surpass the narrow confines of time and body.

There is no tomorrow, there is only today. And those who sacrifice their own today to better people's tomorrow, get indelibly embedded upon the fabric of time in golden letters.

> Yarın yok, sadece bugün var;
> Benim her gün insanlara kurban.
> Çünkü herkes bencil yaşarsa,
> Güneş yok, sadece yaralar yarın.

26. I'm Impossible (Sonnet 1272)

I'm Impossible
(Sonnet 1272)

I don't need to play word games,
to say, impossible means I am possible;
my existence is epitome of the impossible.
I don't make plans, I make purpose,
then the purpose plans me, into unstoppable.

Does that mean, loneliness doesn't bother me,
Of course it does - it makes the torture worse.
Anybody who says, they enjoy loneliness,
is either lying or plain narcissistic retard.

But then again, just when I feel super gloomy,
I remember my responsibility to my world family.
Time and again, my purpose drags me out,
Electrifying my veins with incorruptible duty.

¡Viva la humanidad, viva la familia mundial!
Long live humanity, long live world family!
Whenever you are down, take refuge in purpose;
Your purpose will reawaken your invincibility.

27. Pani, Agua, Water Sonnet

Iman Insaniyat, Mazhab Muhabbat
(Pani, Agua, Water Sonnet, 1273)

In some circles, I am called a genius,
Yet the only genius I know of is service.
In other circles, I am branded fraud,
Yet the only fraud I know of is prejudice.

Saying, you've explored my work,
after spending an evening scrolling
through a few quotes, is like saying,
you've climbed Mount Everest,
after spending an evening scrolling
through pictures of the Himalayas.

Yet I can tell you who I am,
I don't need a million lines but one.
Iman insaniyat, mazhab muhabbat*;
Pani, agua, water, it's all one.

Take my Bible, Koran & Vedas,
Take my Origin of Species.
Throw me to the fires of hell,
My life will still smell of roses.

(*faith humanity, religion love)

28. Bible, Vedas, Koran
(Sonnet 1274)

Bible, Vedas, Koran
(Sonnet 1274)

Take my Bible,
Take my Vedas;
Take my Koran,
Take my Suttas;
Take my Darwin,
Take my creation;
Take my Aquinas,
Take my Atom;
Take my myths,
Take my reason;
Take my facts,
Take my fiction;
Take the whole lot,
I'll still be human.
My humanity thrives beyond
all dualities of facts and fiction.

29. Sonnet 1275

Sonnet 1275

The tendency of this or that,
will ultimately be the end of us.
Till you learn to side with humanity,
all your faith and facts are useless.
Fundamentalists peddle intolerance through faith,
Militant atheists peddle divide through facts.
Unless they both grow up into human beings,
Both are equally and unequivocally backwards.
All borders imposed on mind are primitive,
Borders that keep people apart from people.
With all your intellect how can you still not see,
Without heart's affection intellect makes sheeple!
Obsessing over faith, facts or nation,
disconnected from heart, is sign of savagery.
The game is abreak - long you've been sheep;
Isn't it time to stand up, and practice humanity!

30. Topnut, DOD Sonnet

Topnut, DOD Sonnet (1276)

Take a fancy celebrity,
put them in military uniform,
suddenly everybody is a patriot.
That's how primitive this world is,
everybody yells about world peace,
while living in militarist gutter.
The best propaganda is one that,
does not feel like propaganda;
Best way to legally recruit terrorists,
is to portray terrorism as valor.
Best way to sustain the revenues of war,
is to showcase war as peace-intervention.
Till you grow up and denounce all militarism,
don't you dare call yourself a civilized human!
We scientists, doctors, nurses and teachers,
forget self-preservation for life-preservation,
while primitive civilians of a primitive planet,
throw all that away, hypnotized by patriotism.

31. Are Soldiers Terrorists

Now we're confronted with a severe question.

Are soldiers terrorists?

Well, whether soldiers are terrorists, depends on which side of the border you are speaking from. Your soldiers are terrorist to the other side, their soldiers are terrorist to you. Fact of the matter is, soldiers are not the problem - they are merely pawn - real culprit of terror is nationalist state.

Doctors don't fight each other in the name of healthcare to fight disease - they fight together as one entity against the disease. And yet, states fight each other in the name of peace, each thinking that the other is the disease - thus they equally co-manufacture the greatest disease of all - war.

Now tell me? Who is the terrorist?

Once you understand this, at the core of your being, the path will unfold on its own.

Hard fact of the matter is, there will always be some sort of fringe element to our human society, which could only be dealt with armed intervention - but why should armed intervention be the very bedrock of the national psyche!

I'll say it to you plainly - in a civilized world, military is not a matter of pride, it's a matter of shame. In a primitive world, national strength is proportional to its military budget, whereas in a civilized world, national backwardness is proportional to its military budget.

If every nation kept their defense budget to the lowest and education budget to the highest, there wouldn't be any terrorism in the world. Show me a nation with a huge defense budget, I'll show you a retarded nation. Show me a nation with a huge education budget, I'll show you a nation of the future.

You know why? Because, education is the ultimate defense policy - education is the highest form of defense - that makes the very narrative of defense and offense obsolete - and that's when peace prevails.

BIBLIOGRAPHY

Archer M., (2000), Being Human: The Problem of Agency. Cambridge University Press.

Adolphs R (2003) Cognitive neuroscience of human social behaviour. Nature Rev Neurosci 4: 165–178.

Adolphs R, Tranel D, Damasio AR (2003) Dissociable neural systems for recognizing emotions. Brain Cogn 52: 61–69.

Andresen, Jensine, and Robert Forman, eds. Cognitive Models and Spiritual Maps. Bowling Green, Ohio: Imprint Academic, 2000.

Bernstein R.J., (1971), Praxis and Action: Contemporary Philosophies of Human Activity. Philadelphia: University of Pennsylvania Press.

Bernstein R.J., (1976), The Restructuring Social and Political Thought.

Bogen, J.E.(1995a), 'On the neurophysiology of consciousness: Part I. An overview', Consciousness and Cognition, 4.

Bogen, J.E. (1995b), 'On the neurophysiology of consciousness: Part II. Constraining the semantic problem', Consciousness and Cognition, 4.

Bremner, J. D., R. Soufer, et al. (2001). "Gender differences in cognitive and neural correlates of remembrance of emotional words." Psychopharmacol Bull 35 (3).

Brothers, L. (2002). The social brain: A project for integrating primate behavior and neurophysiology in a new domain. In J. T. Cacioppo et al. (Eds.), Foundations in neuroscience. Cambridge, MA: MIT Press.

Buss, D. D. (2003). Evolutionary Psychology: The New Science of Mind, 2nd ed. New York: Allyn & Bacon.

Buss, D. M. (1989). "Conflict between the sexes: Strategic interference and the evocation of anger and upset." J Pers Soc Psychol 56 (5).

Buss, D. M. (1995). "Psychological sex differences. Origins through sexual selection." Am Psychol 50 (3).

Buss, D. M., and D. P. Schmitt (1993). "Sexual strategies theory: An evolutionary perspective on human mating." Psychol Rev 100 (2).

Chomsky Noam, (2016) Who Rules the World?

Churchland, P.S. (1986), Neurophilosophy (Cambridge, MA: The MIT Press).

Churchland, P.S. & Ramachandran, V.S. (1993), 'Filling in: Why Dennett is wrong', in Dennett and His Critics:

Demystifying Mind, ed. B. Dahlbom (Oxford: Blackwell Scientific Press).

Churchland, P.S., Ramachandran, V.S. & Sejnowski, T.J. (1994), 'A critique of pure vision', in Large- scale Neuronal Theories of the Brain, ed. C. Koch & J.L. Davis (Cambridge, MA: The MIT Press).

Crick, F. (1994), The Astonishing Hypothesis: The Scientific Search for the Soul (New York: Simon and Schuster).

Crick, F. (1996), 'Visual perception: rivalry and consciousness', Nature, 379.

Crick, F. & Koch, C. (1992), 'The problem of consciousness', Scientific American, 267.

d'Aquili, Eugene. "Senses of Reality in Science and Religion." Zygon 17, no 4 (1982)

d'Aquili, Eugene. "The Biopsychological Determinants of Religious Ritual Behavior." Zygon 10, no. 1 (1975)

d'Aquili, Eugene. "The Myth-Ritual Complex: A Biogenetic Structural Analysis." Zygon 18, no. 3 (1983)

d'Aquili, Eugene, and Andrew Newberg. The Mystical Mind: Probing the Biology of Religious Experience. Minneapolis: Fortress Press, 1999.

Damasio, A. (1994) Descartes' Error: Emotion, Reason and the Human Brain. New York, Putnams.

Damasio, A. (1999) The Feeling of What Happens: Body, Emotion and the Making of Consciousness. London, Heinemann.

Darwin, C. (1859) On the Origin of Species by Means of Natural Selection. London, Murray.

Darwin, C. (1871) The Descent of Man and Selection in Relation to Sex. London, John Murray.

Dawkins, R. (1976) The Selfish Gene. Oxford, Oxford University Press; a new edition, with additional material, was published in 1989.

Dewhurst, Kenneth, and A. W. Beard. "Sudden Religious Conversions in Temporal Lobe Epilepsy." British Journal of Psychiatry 117 (1970)

Dewhurst K, Beard AW. Sudden religious conversions in temporal lobe epilepsy. 1970 Epilepsy Behav 2003

Devinsky O, Lai G. Spirituality and religion in epilepsy. Epilepsy Behav 2008.

E. Horvitz, "One Hundred Year Study on Artificial Intelligence: Reflections and Framing," ed: Stanford University, 2014.

Eckhart Meister, Selected Writings

Farah, M.J. (1989), 'The neural basis of mental imagery', Trends in Neurosciences, 10.

Freud, S. "Selected papers on hysteria and other psychoneuroses" Journal of Nervous and Mental Disease 1909.

Freud, S. "The Origin and Development of Psychoanalysis", 1910

Freud, S. "Psychopathology of everyday life", 1914

Freud, S. "Beyond the Pleasure Principle", 1920

Frith, C.D. & Dolan, R.J. (1997), 'Abnormal beliefs: Delusions and memory', Paper presented at the May, 1997, Harvard Conference on Memory and Belief.

Gay, Volney, ed. Neuroscience and Religion. Plymouth, UK: Lexington Books, 2009.

Gazzaniga, M. S. (1985). The social brain. New York: Basic Books.

Gazzaniga, M.S. (1993), 'Brain mechanisms and conscious experience', Ciba Foundation Symposium, 174.

Geschwind N. "Behavioural changes in temporal lobe epilepsy". Psychol Med. 1979.

Gellhorn, E., Kiely, W.F. "Mystical states of consciousness: neurophysiological and clinical aspects." J Nerv Ment Dis. 1972;154:399-405.

Gilbert SL, Dobyns WB, Lahn BT (2005) Genetic links between brain development and brain evolution. Nat Rev Genet 6.

Gray JA. The Psychology of Fear and Stress. 2nd ed. New York, NY: Cambridge University Press; 1988.

Gloor, P. (1992), 'Amygdala and temporal lobe epilepsy', in The Amygdala: Neurobiological Aspects of Emotion, Memory and Mental

Dysfunction, ed J.P. Aggleton (New York: Wiley-Liss).

Gross CG, Rocha-Miranda CE, Bender DB (1972) Visual properties of neurons in the inferotemporal cortex of the macaque. J Neurophysiol 35: 96–111.

Guevara Che, The Motorcycle Diaries, 1992

Hardy, G. H. (1940). Ramanujan. Cambridge: Cambridge University Press.

Hall, Daniel, Keith Meador, and Harold Koenig. "Measuring Religiousness in Health Research: Review and Critique." Journal of Religion and Health 47, no. 2 (2008)

Harris, Sam, Jonas Kaplan, Ashley Curiel, Susan Bookheimer, Marco Iacoboni, and Mark Cohen. "The Neural Correlates of Religious and Nonreligious Belief." PLoS One 4, no. 10 (October 1, 2009)

Halgren, E. (1992), 'Emotional neurophysiology of the amygdala within the context of human cognition', in The Amygdala: Neurobiological Aspects of Emotion, Memory and Mental Dysfunction, ed J.P. Aggleton (New York: Wiley-Liss).

Halligan PW, Fink GR, Marshal JC, Vallar G. 2003. Spatial cognition: evidence from visual neglect. Trends Cogn Sci.

Handbook of Emotions, Edited by Michael Lewis, Jeannette M. Haviland-Jones, and Lisa Feldman Barrett, The Guilford Press; 3rd edition (2010).

Hameroff, S.R. and Penrose, R. (1996) Conscious events as orchestrated space-time selections. Journal of Consciousness Studies 3(1), 36-53; also reprinted in J. Shear (ed.) (1997) Explaining Consciousness-The Hard Problem. Cambridge, MA, MIT Press, 177-95.

Harding, D.E. (1961) On Having no Head: Zen and the Re-Discovery of the Obvious. London, Buddhist Society.

Hardy, A. (1979) The Spiritual Nature of Man: A Study of Contemporary Religious Experience. Oxford, Clarendon Press.

Harre, R. and Gillett, G. (1994) The Discursive Mind. Thousand Oaks, CA, Sage.

Haugeland, J. (ed.) (1997) Mind Design II: Philosophy, Psychology, Artificial Intelligence. Cambridge, MA, MIT Press.

Hauser, M.D. (2000) Wild Minds: What Animals Really Think. New York, Henry Holt and Co.; London, Penguin.

Hilgard, E.R. (1986) Divided Consciousness: Multiple Controls in Human Thought and Action. New York, Wiley.

Hilton, E.N., Lundberg, T.R. Transgender Women in the Female Category of Sport: Perspectives on Testosterone Suppression and Performance Advantage. Sports Med 51, 199–214 (2021).

Hitler, Adolf. Mein Kampf, 1925

Hodgson, R. (1891) A case of double consciousness. Proceedings of the Society for Psychical Research 7, 221-58.

Hofstadter, D.R. and Dennett, D.C. (eds) (1981) The Mind's I: Fantasies and Reflections on Self and Soul. London, Penguin.

Holland, J. (ed.) (2001) Ecstasy: The Complete Guide: A Comprehensive Look at the Risks and Benefits of MDMA. Rochester, VT, Park Street Press.

Holmes, D.S. (1987) The influence of meditation versus rest on physiological arousal. In M. West (ed.)

The Psychology of Meditation. Oxford, Clarendon Press, 81-103.

Holmstrom, David. 1992, Christian Science Monitor

Holloway RL (1996) Evolution of the human brain. In: Lock A, Peters CR (eds) Handbook of human symbolic evolution. Oxford University Press, Oxford

Jeannerod M (1988) The neural and behavioural organization of goal-directed movements. Clarendon Press, Oxford.

Johnson-Frey SH, Maloof FR, Newman-Norlund R, Farrer C, Inati S, Grafton ST (2003) Actions or hand-objects interactions? Human inferior frontal cortex and action observation. Neuron 39: 1053–1058.

Jackson, F. (1982) Epiphenomenal qualia. Philosophical Quarterly 32, 127-36.

James, W. (1890) The Principles of Psychology (2 volumes). London, Macmillan.

James, W. (1902) The Varieties of Religious Experience: A Study in Human Nature. New York and London, Longmans, Green and Co.

Jansen, K. (2001) Ketamine: Dreams and Realities. Sarasota, FL, Multidisciplinary Association for Psychedelic Studies.

Jay, M. (ed.) (1999) Artificial Paradises: A Drugs Reader. London, Penguin.

Jaynes, J. (1976) The Origin of Consciousness in the Breakdown of the Bicameral Mind. New York, Houghton Mifflin.

Kandel, E. R. In Search of Memory: The Emergence of a New Science of Mind, W. W. Norton & Company (2007).

Kandel E. R. Schwartz JH, Jessel TM. Principles of neural sciences. New York; McGraw Hill, 2000.

Kanwisher, N. (2001) Neural events and perceptual awareness. Cognition 79, 89-113; also reprinted inS. Dehaene (ed.) The Cognitive Neuroscience of Consciousness. Cambridge, MA, MIT Press, 89-113.

Kihlstrom, J.F. (1996) Perception without awareness of what is perceived, learning without awareness of what is learned. In M. Velmans (ed.) The Science of Consciousness. London, Routledge, 23-46.

Kosslyn, S.M. (1980) Image and Mind. Cambridge, MA, Harvard University Press.

Kosslyn, S.M. (1988) Aspects of a cognitive neuroscience of mental imagery. Science 240, 1621-6.

Kjaer, Troels, Camilla Bertelsen, Paola Piccini, David Brooks, Jorgen Alving, and Hans Lou. "Increased Dopamine Tone during Meditation- Induced Change of Consciousness." Cognitive Brain Research 13, no. 2 (April 2002)

Kölmel HW. 1985. Complex visual hallucinations in the hemianopic field. J Neurol Neurosurg Psychiatry.

Koenig, Harold. "Research on Religion, Spirituality, and Mental Health: A Review." Canadian Journal of Psychiatry 54, no. 5 (May 2009)

Koenig, Harold, ed. Handbook of Religion and Mental Health. San Diego, CA: Academic Press, 1998

Kraepelin E. Psychiatry: A Textbook for Students and Physicians. New York, NY: Science History Publications; 1990.

Lauglin, Charles, John McManus, and Eugene d'Aquili. Brain, Symbol, and Experience. 2nd ed. New York: Columbia University Press, 1992

Lakoff, G. and M. Johnson (1999). Philosophy in the flesh. Basic Books: New York.

LeDoux, J. E. (1996). The emotional brain. New York: Simon & Schuster.

LeDoux, J.E. (1992), 'Emotion and the amygdala', in The Amygdala: Neurobiological Aspects of Emo- tion, Memory and Mental Dysfunction, ed J.P. Aggleton (New York: Wiley-Liss).

Levin, D.T. and Simons, D.J. (1997) Failure to detect changes to attended objects in motion pictures. Psychonomic Bulletin and Review 4, 501-6.

Levine,J. (1983) Materialism and qualia: the explanatory gap. Pacific Philosophical Quarterly 64, 354-61.

Levine,J. (2001) Purple Haze: The Puzzle of Consciousness. New York, Oxford University Press. Levine, S. (1979) A Gradual Awakening. New York, Doubleday.

Levinson, B.W. (1965) States of awareness during general anaesthesia. British Journal of Anaesthesia 37, 544-6.

Lewicki, P., Czyzewska, M. and Hoffman, H. (1987) Unconscious acquisition of complex procedural knowledge. Journal of Experimental Psychology: Learning, Memory and Cognition 13, 523-30.

Naskar, Abhijit. "What is Mind?", 2016

Naskar, Abhijit. "Love, God & Neurons: Memoir of A Scientist who found himself by getting lost", 2016

Naskar, Abhijit. "Principia Humanitas", 2017

Naskar, Abhijit. "We Are All Black: A Treatise on Racism", 2017

Naskar, Abhijit. "Either Civilized or Phobic: A Treatise on Homosexuality", 2017

Naskar, Abhijit. "Build Bridges not Walls: In the name of Americana", 2018

Naskar, Abhijit. "Citizens of Peace: Beyond the Savagery of Sovereignty", 2019

Naskar, Abhijit. "The Constitution of The United Peoples of Earth", 2019

Naskar, Abhijit. "Mission Reality", 2019

Naskar, Abhijit. "Good Scientist: When Science and Service Combine", 2020

Newberg, Andrew, and Jeremy Iversen. "The Neural Basis of the Complex Mental Task of Meditation: Neurotransmitter and Neurochemical Considerations." Medical Hypotheses 61, no. 2 (2003).

Newberg, Andrew. "How God Changes Your Brain: An Introduction to Jewish Neurotheology", CCAR

Journal: The Reform Jewish Quarterly, Winter 2016.

Newberg, Andrew, and Stephanie Newberg. "A Neuropsychological Perspective on Spiritual Development." In Handbook of Spiritual Development in Childhood and Adolescence, edited by Eugene Roehlkepartain, Pamela King, Linda Wagener, and Peter Benson. London: Sage Publications, Inc., 2005

Newberg, Andrew. "The Neurotheology Link An Intersection Between Spirituality and Health", Alternative and Complimentary Therapies, Vol 21 No 1, February 2015.

Newberg, Andrew, Nancy Wintering, Dharma Khalsa, Hannah Roggenkamp, and Mark Waldman. "Meditation Effects on Cognitive Function and Cerebral Blood Flow in Subjects with Memory Loss: A Preliminary Study." Journal of Alzheimer's Disease 20, no. 2 (2010)

Nash, M. (1995), 'Glimpses of the mind', Time.

Nesse RM. Proximate and evolutionary studies of anxiety, stress and depression: synergy at the interface. Neurosci Biobehav Rev. 1999;23:895-903.

Nicolelis, Miguel. (2011) "Beyond Boundaries: The New Neuroscience of Connecting Brains with Machines---and How It Will Change Our Lives", Times Books

O'Hara, K. and Scutt, T. (1996) There is no hard problem of consciousness. Journal of Consciousness Studies 3(4), 290-302, reprinted in J. Shear (ed.) (1997) Explaining Consciousness. Cambridge, MA, MIT Press, 69-82.

O'Regan, J.K. and Noe, A. (2001) A sensorimotor account of vision and visual consciousness. Behavioral and Brain Sciences 24(5), 883-917.

Ornstein, R.E. (1977) The Psychology of Consciousness (2nd edn). New York, Harcourt.

Ornstein, R.E. (1986) The Psychology of Consciousness (3rd edn). New York, Pehguin.

Ornstein, R.E. (1992) The Evolution of Consciousness. New York, Touchstone.

Penfield W, Faulk ME (1955) The insula: further observations on its function. Brain 78: 445– 470.

Penrose, R. (1994), Shadows of the Mind (Oxford: Oxford University Press).

Penrose, R. (1989), The Emperor's New Mind: Concerning Computers, Minds and The Laws of Physics (Oxford: Oxford University Press).

Persinger, "'I would kill in God's name' role of sex, weekly church attendance, report of a religious experience and limbic lability" Perceptual and Motor Skills 1997.

Persinger "Experimental simulation of the God experience" Neurotheology 2003.

Persinger, Corradini, Clement, Keaney, et al "Neurotheology and its convergence with neuroquantology" NeuroQuantology 2010.

Persinger. "The neuropsychiatry of paranormal experiences". J Neuropsychiatry Clin Neurosci 2001.

Persinger. "Neuropsychological bases of god beliefs", New York: Praeger, 1987

Persinger. "Temporal lobe epileptic signs and correlative behaviors displayed by normal populations", Journal of General Psychology, 1986

Perry BD, Pollard R. Homeostasis, stress, trauma, and adaptation. A neurodevelopmental view of childhood trauma. Child Adolesc Psychiatr Clin N Am. 1998;7:33.

Ramachandran VS. Behavioral and magnetoencephalographic correlates of plasticity in the adult human brain. Proc Natl Acad Sci USA 1993; 90: 10413–20.

Ramachandran VS. Plasticity and functional recovery in neurology. Clin Med 2005; 5: 368–73.

Rock I, Victor J. Vision and touch: an experimentally created conflict between the two senses. Science 1964; 143: 594–6.

Roberts, TA; Smalley, J; Ahrendt, D (December 2020). "Effect of gender affirming hormones on athletic performance in transwomen and transmen: implications for sporting organisations and legislators". British Journal of Sports Medicine. 55 (11): 577–583

Royet JP, Plailly J, Delon-Martin C, Kareken DA, Segebarth C (2003) fMRI of emotional responses to odors: influence of hedonic valence and judgment, handedness, and gender. Neuroimage 20: 713–728.

Rozin R Haidt J and McCauley CR (2000) Disgust. In: Lewis M, Haviland-Jones JM (eds) Handbook of Emotion. 2nd Edition. Guilford Press, New York, pp 637–653.

Saxe R, Carey S, Kanwisher N (2004) Understanding other minds: linking developmental psychology and functional neuroimaging. Annu Rev Psychol 55: 87–124.

S. J. Russell and P. Norvig, Artificial intelligence: a modern approach (3rd edition): Prentice Hall, 2009.

Singer T, Seymour B, O'Doherty J, Kaube H, Dolan RJ, Frith CD (2004) Empathy for pain involves the affective but not the sensory components of pain. Science 303: 1157–1162.

Smith A (1759) The theory of moral sentiments (ed. 1976). Clarendon Press, Oxford.

Schilling, Vincent. 2017, indian country today

Stein, Stephen K. 2017, The Sea in World History: Exploration, Travel, and Trade

Tesla N. "My Inventions", 1919

T. R. Society, "Machine learning: the power and promise of computers that learn by example," ed. The Royal Society, 2017.

Tomasello M, Call J (1997) Primate cognition. Oxford University Press, Oxford